The Real Deal: The Jou.. ..

Brittney J. McCurry

The Real Deal: The Journey

Edited By: Dr. Tammie McCurry

Copyright©2016 Brittney McCurry

ISBN-13: 978-1535483209 (CreateSpace-Assigned)
ISBN-10: 1535483202

Printed in the United States of America.

*A phenomenal woman, my god-grandmother, **Johnnie Mae Sellers**. Absent from Earth but your soul will forever live. I will always hold you close to my heart. This book is dedicated to you and everything you've done and the lives you've touched.*

To my heavenly Father Jesus Christ for without him there would be no me! Thank you God for instilling this precious gift in me. Most of all thank you for never leaving me even when I may have deserved your grace. For you I live.

TABLE OF CONTENTS
PREFACE-----------DEDICATION
ACKNOWLEDGMENTS
WHAT A WOMAN

LOVE:
MOM
DAD
LOVE
THE SPECIAL LOVE
COULD THIS BE
I WANT YOU TO KNOW
LOST LOVE
A TRUE FRIEND
IT TAKES THREE
A BROKEN HEART
MY MISTAKE
SPECIAL FEELING
THE DIFFERENCE BETWEEN THE
TWO B vs M
THE DIFFERENCE BETWEEN THE
TWO G vs W

MEMORIES:
DISTANT DAD
IF I COULD I WOULD
RACE
BACK IN THE DAY
IT WILL BE OKAY
SUNRISE TO SUNSET
USE TO BE
NOBODY TO SOMEBODY
A FRIEND I CHERISH
IT'S OKAY...IT WAS TIME
I'M NOT WORRIED

LIFE:
WHEN I THINK
LIFE
HOLD ON
THE TIME OF MY LIFE
LAST RIDE
BECAUSE OF YOU

IF I ONLY HAD A CLUE
THE TEACHER
BREAKING NEWS
I WONDER
DON'T BE FOOLED
THIS GIRL
DECEPTION
SILENT CRIES: ELI
SILENT CRIES: JENNIFER
SILENT CRIES: BRIAN&BRIANNA
I'M SORRY
3:00PM
COACHES MVP
BATTLING WITHIN
A LESSON LEARNED
YOU DESERVE TO KNOW
THE FINALE
IT'S YOUR LIFE
HOW COME
HELP ME UNDERSTAND

RELIGIOUS:
FINDING MYSELF THROUGH YOU
DEAR LORD
THANK YOU
THE MORNING KEY
IT WILL COME
THE TEST
HEAVEN
CHURCH
ARE YOU A CHRISTIAN?
P.U.S.H
A TURN AROUND ...TO TURN
AWAY

PREFACE

Life (sarcastically laughing)…..Sometimes life gives us lemons and we are supposed to make lemonade out of it. We didn't get the luxury of choosing our lives but we have the ability to change it but it took me awhile to understand that. Bad things happen to good people. We have all heard the quote before. In this book you will travel down various paths that life seems to sometimes take one on whether it be in your spiritual or personal life. How we handle obstacles placed in our way during our journey shows one's ability to persevere.

This book will allow you to put yourself in the shoes of your neighbor, your sister, your brother, your church member and experience the hurdles. You never really know what a person may be going through until you ask. This book is not here to tell you everything will work out how you feel it should, but to reassure you that you are not alone and after the storm the sun does shine. This book is an outlet better yet a voice for those who have encountered similar situations or know of someone who had to deal with the same hardship.

Like listening to a song when you are hurting it is always nice to know someone else out there understands. As the reader you will be able to relate to at least one poem if not more. I hope this book inspires you to be real with your feelings and never give in or up when adversity faces you.

"Getting over a painful experience is much like crossing monkey bars. You have to let go at some point in order to move forward"---Unknown

God Bless.

DEDICATION

This book is dedicated to my loving and caring parents, Michael and Tammie McCurry. Thank you for allowing me to be who I am and express myself. Thank you for always being that wall I needed to lean on when things not always going right. Thank you for raising me into the woman I am today! Thank you for being my backbone through it all. I love you unconditionally.

To my five young ladies, Alyssa, Jasmine, Takia, Mikala, and Ashley. I am so blessed to have you in my life. Our sisterly bond has grown over the years. No matter what I will always be there for you girls. Each of you play a major role in my life because without you girls by my side I would have given up on things so easily but you girls keep me going!

To my grandparents, Earlene Ross and Willie and Ruby Nell McCurry. You have always said, "Practice makes perfect" and "if you put your mind to it you can do it". I want to thank you for always being there to pat me on the shoulder. Thank you for instilling such strong morals and values into my life. Thank you from the bottom of my heart.

ACKNOWLEDGEMENTS

With special thanks:

To my loving parents, Michael and Tammie McCurry, for all the help you gave me, for all the encouragement you pushed toward me. From the day I was brought into this world God knew what he was doing when he gave me you two. Thank you for walking two steps behind me when I tried to do things on my own.

To my sisters, thanks for always taking time out of your busy schedules to listen to my poems and to encourage me when I would get discouraged. Thank you so much you don't know how much you've impacted this dream.

To my grandparents; Earlene Ross; and Willie and Ruby Nell McCurry for always giving me those words of encouragement to keep me going and keep. And for telling me, "Don't ever let anyone tell you that you'll never be something because you already are".

To my 10th grade Biology teacher, Tashara King, I want to thank you for being there for me whenever I needed you. Only you will know how much I appreciate who you are to me. All the encouragement through the hard times blessed me the most. Words cannot describe how thankful I am to God that He allowed you to come into my life. I thank and love you with all my heart.

Thank you to three extraordinary women who helped me through junior high school and have been my mentors. First, Mrs. Shawndra Johnson my computer teacher for always believing in me and always telling me, "I know you will be something excellent when you are older; just keep walking with the Lord". To Mrs. Kimberly Audaine my 7th grade English teacher for always encouraging me to enter into the poetic competitions and always giving me that pat on the back and telling me, "Great Writing". Last, certainly not least to my 8th grade Math teacher Ms. Maya Stubbs for making me stronger spiritually, mentally, and physically.

To my Pastor Terry and First Lady Jevonnah Ellison. Thank you for setting a solid foundation in my spiritual growth. Thank you for all your encouragement and motivation to never give up even when the odds were against me.

To all of my friends and family members; thank you all for supporting me in your various roles. I appreciate each and every one of you.

WHAT A WOMAN

Sitting here thinking to myself this
can't be true.
I'm in denial that I actually lost
you.

It seems like it was yesterday you
were getting on to me
About grades. Yes, those were the
days I'm sure everyone
Will agree.

You see you were what most
women are trying to be. No one
Is perfect but to me God molded
you close to be.

Even though this is hard I know
now you are pain free. Living in the
sky
Looking down on me. Most people
may say you passed away at a
young
Age, but little do they know your
life was far from vain.

You see the years God gave you;
you enjoyed them while they
lasted. Some
Will never be able to say before I
went home I was able to help save
someone's
Soul.

Nor will they be able to say before
I closed my eyes I helped to
changed peoples
Lives. Ms. Sellers you are the
epitome of what I want to be and
what others
Want their children to be.

I remember what you told me the
other night so I guess I should now
share that
Insight.

"Never give up nor give in because
if you do; you have allowed the
devil to win. Sin is
A sickness of its own…take your
problems to God and then leave
them alone.

When something isn't right just
continue to fight and when you feel
oh so tired simply
Think of me and keep doing your
best because it's not until the Lord
comes to you and
Says, "My child it's time". Only
then you may rest!

To everyone that may know me or
whose lives I have touched. Do me
a favor and thank our Savior for
I am now in a better place in much
better shape.

Grieving is ok but don't let your
emotions override you. Be happy
and celebrate for I am sitting
Upon cloud nine and I am doing
just fine."

Ms. Seller's one last thing I want
you to know because of you I know
now I have no reason to complain.
I know now that I need to live the
right way. Thank you for
everything especially for just being
you and

With that said I love you and that
will always be true!

"Love is just a word until someone special gives it meaning"
-Unknown

MOM

Dear Mom,
I've never been good at public speaking so I'm writing you this letter.

A lot of people wouldn't know that you had me at a young age of 19. I'm sure at the time you had big dreams, but before I continue I must say thank you for having me.

Never did I want, never did I lack and I am grateful for that. Working numerous jobs to come home only to pull a double.

Yes the usual cook and clean....you know all the motherly things. Not once while I was growing up did you complain...well at least not in front of me.

How did you become so strong? Six girls, a husband, a career...yes that's unheard of.

Day in and day out you provided for us. Always there no matter the time or day. You always made a way.

I should tell you more often but I look up to you. Yes ma'am I truly salute you.

With all that you've been through. There's no way you should still be here in your right mind.

I thank God for you. It's something about having purpose. God ordained a woman that He knew would go through what she had to. As Tupac Shakur says, "There's no woman alive that can take my mama's place".

You're like my best friend and I hope that never ends.

Dear Mom, I've never been good at public speaking but if I had to stand in front of a crowd I would say, I am proud to be your child.

DAD

Daddy's girl. Yes that's me. You see growing up I never had to go looking for you because you were always there.

Absentee dad ...what's that. My super hero always had my back. Taught me how to tie my shoes and ride my first bike.

Daddy's girl. Yes that's me. When I was 13 my dad took me on my first date. He taught me how a man should treat me and never settle for anything less than that.

The most insightful and humble man I know. God showed me favor when you and mom became equally yoked.

Daddy's girl. Yes that's definitely me. The first born, your seed. Striving every day to make sure you're proud of me. Never wanting to disappoint you because you never let me down.

I never understood how other kids wouldn't want their dad's around. I love my dad with all my heart.

From finish to start you've never left me in the dark. You taught me

right from wrong so here's your song.
Your eagerness and willingness are what I like best. I want You to know God said you have past the previous test.

Unfortunately, the devil never seems to rest. But he should realize the man we serve is the best.

Even though the devil has tried numerous times to take your life ...our God put up a bigger fight because he wasn't through with you yet.

So this is it ...devil we put you on notice you have tried your last attempt.
Daddy's girl, yes my dad is my first hero.

LOVE

*Love… where have you been? I
thought my life was about to end.
When I saw you I knew it was about
to begin because God sent*

*Me you. Yes, my love is true
especially to you. Do you know how
I know our love is true?*

*Because when I go through you do
too. When I needed a hand I knew
you were just the man to
understand.*

*When I need a shoulder to lean on,
you're always there when I call.*

That's why my love is so strong!

THE SPECIAL LOVE

*You may wonder what love is or
how it may work. You may wonder
if the saying, love at first sight is
true.*

*You may find yourself lost in a
tunnel and you don't
Know which way is out.*

*The question you constantly beat
yourself up about; how can I find
that special love?*

*You have searched on every corner
to see if that love was hiding, but
still no love there.*

*There's one way and one answer to
that question. So please let me
guide you in the right direction you
need to ask this person*

*You may know very well. If you
don't know who let me help you out
a little.*

This person is you!

COULD THIS BE

What should I do now? I don't know why, but every time I think of you all I want to do is cry.

I tried to hide the way I feel and keep my words unspoken with my lips sealed.

I can't help but think was our love real or was it one of those quick deals.

I gave up on us when I didn't want to try anymore and yes that was my big mistake.

When I tried to move on I still hear my little song, "now you're gone, but I still love you".

How could this be I feel like you're still a part of me, can't you see! I think we were meant to be!

I WANT YOU TO KNOW

I've been having a little trouble finding myself. When I look into the mirror I see the reflection of someone I want to live

Up to be. I know no one is perfect, but I think God has molded you close to be.

When I look at you; you show you never give up. Even when you may be down you never show a frown.

You told me you endure many trials, but you just don't show that type of lifestyle.

You always let me know growing up is never easy. I learned from you that friends might come and go but there will always

Be one at the end of the road. You always encourage me to do right and keep God in sight.

Always wanting what's best and telling me to do what works for me.

I can't believe God let me trust in someone I barely knew. I had no clue, but I'm glad it was you.

Without hesitating for a second I told you my life and without judging you told me everything would be alright.

You let me know that someone else is going through too. So I wouldn't feel so blue.

<u>LOST LOVE</u>

My best friend, my superman we're holding hands. You tell me you love me continually.

You told me I was your world, yes me, I was your girl. "Sometimes you have to hurt the ones you love", is what you said to me as you looked into my eyes.

Confused and puzzled we kissed goodnight.

Before you left you seemed as if you wanted to cry, but you told me a lie and said everything will be alright.

Little did I know that was our last good-bye. I had no clue that you wanted to die.

Now I'm sitting here asking myself why? How do I deal without you…? I really don't know what to do.

You were my friend the one I confided in. Our love was so strong…maybe I was the one that did something wrong.

That night I received some horrible news …I can't believe I had to lose you.

You were there through my pain…you were there to cheer me up when things weren't going my way.

Why didn't anyone tell me love could hurt so badly? We made plans to be a family.

I can't help but remember the good days when I had no room to complain.

Now it's too late to say the things I wanted to say. That beautiful day was the last time I saw your handsome face.

From my heart I wish we didn't have to depart, but my superman, my best friend now that you're gone I'm truly

Lost without you. You convinced me life is worth living. Now that you're gone here's your little song, "my love for you will last

To the end". You were my companion and my very best friend. My superman you will be missed so I leave you with this one

…. Last…. kiss.

A TRUE FRIEND

*I'm not the easiest person to get
along with,
But no matter what you always
stick with me.
I shared my deepest secrets with
you that I knew
I couldn't tell anyone else.*

*No matter what you always knew
what to say.
Always having your arms out for
me and an ear
To listen out for me when you knew
things
Weren't going right.*

*When I got into trouble you always
tried to
Get me out. See you are a true
friend; got my back
Through thick and thin.*

*Of course we had our ups and
downs but it didn't
Do anything but bring us closer
together. When I hurt
You felt my pain. When I cry you
cry, but you kept it bundled inside.*

*A true friend I recommend to
everyone. You're
Like the big sister I never had and
I'm glad
You're my
Best friend!*

IT TAKES THREE

*Take my hand and guide me
through the sand.
Take my hand and be a man.
Please take my hand*

*And usher me into that special
land. We must move
At a fast pace to start the race.
Look into my face this*

*Is a non-winning case. Let's walk
together it takes
Two to make a couple, but three to
make a great team.*

*In order to win the race in first
place we must give up some
In order to gain. This may sound
lame, but in order to win*

*The game everyone must
participate. That means you, me
And the Lord in order to make the
winning score.*

*So don't give up now the race may
have ended, but the
Journey has just begun.*

*We have won the fight, but the
battle is on the way.
So let it be known we are going all
the way when war*

Comes in our marriage way!

A BROKEN HEART

What happened between us; all was going well.
We started off kind of rough, but when our eyes locked there was no turning back.

I've been hurt so many times I was scared to love you. For some reason I couldn't resist...I guess I just wanted to take that kind of risk.

We shared some good times that could last forever. We had our moments when we couldn't stand to be near each other.

At the end of the day we made up as if nothing had ever happened.. I knew we would have our ups and downs, but why so many in this amount of time.

See this is why I was afraid to love you because
Somehow I knew I was going to end up losing you.
I was ready to commit when you weren't.

Now I'm starting to regret the things I did, the thoughts I shared, the emotions I let you feel, and the love I was beginning to give.

You made promises to me that you knew you couldn't keep and I was dumb enough to believe we were meant to be.

I gave you the key to my heart, but now I have to change the locks, because you and me are no more.

I guess it's true "never say hello if you really mean good-bye". In other words don't say, "I love you" unless you really want to make me cry!

MY MISTAKE

This is the hardest thing I think I had to do. To come and talk to you and tell you what I've been through.

You see I have shut you out of certain parts of my life. So in other words our relationship has been built around lies.

Don't get me wrong I love you with my whole heart, but I have to confess something's happened while we were a part.

I know I use to ask you were you ready to commit, when I should have been asking myself because I simply was not ready for it.

When we first started dating I felt I had waited long enough so you must be the one. Without doubting myself I went on.

Things have been great. You make me laugh in good times and bad. Everyone has flaws no one is perfect, yes that is true, but I have taken that quote too deep in truth.

Not to be conceited but I am a good catch and sometimes I can't seem to resist the attention that I get.

Now I must reminisce and tell you this. I've been approached many times, but for some reason this time I could not stand my ground.

One thing led to another. It started off oh so innocent, but then things got heated and I cheated. I never meant to hurt you those were never my intentions. Like I told you before I love you with my soul, but that night I wasn't thinking right.

Yes I know I need to redefine what I call love. Nothing can justify what I have done. So I understand if you don't want us to continue, but let me say this.

From the beginning I knew you were the one to change my world. You see I was so happy to be your girl.

Things got rocky, but they are supposed to and we made it through. I'm sorry for this mistake I have made and I'm willing to fix it no matter how long it takes.

<u>A SPECIAL FEELING</u>

I've been in so many relationships in the past I just knew this one would not last. I thought this one is no different from the rest.

Never the less you took me at best with your smile and the warm feelings as if I were a child. There's so much I could say but that day I started to feel complete.

That was the day you became a part of me. I felt like the luckiest girl to be a part of your world. You make me happy when things just aren't right. You give me that extra push when I tell you I'm too tired to fight.

You hold my hand when I can't seem to find the light. You are my better half without you it would be hard to last.

When we are together I look in your eyes and I see forever. It's sad it took me this long to find you, but now that you're here I can't image living without you.

No one can ever make me feel the way you do even if they tried. I cannot lie you're one of a kind...and you're mines!

Promise me we will take our time because I want us to last. Thank you for being a part of my life.

Now I can't wait to say "yes I am honored to be your wife".

THE DIFFERENCE BETWEEN THE TWO: BOYS VS MEN

Ladies you should know the difference between the two. A boy and man cannot do the same that the other can do.

A boy is more interested in seeing what you as his girl can do for him, while a man wants to know how he can keep and grow with you.

A boy gets jealous when someone else looks at you, while a man loves to show you to the world for he is confident that he is going home with you.

A boy always wants to know when he can "get some", while a man doesn't mind the wait for he knows when he does get the chance to intertwine with you it will blow his mind away.

A boy tries to hide things from his girl so she won't get mad, while a man knows no one is perfect and apologizes for any disappointment.

A boy will lie until she proves he's wrong, while a man admits, repents, and adjust so it will never happen again.

A boy will be by your side when it's just you two, but when friends are around he will act as if he doesn't even know you. While a man's friends will recognize… before he even introduces you.

A boy will get greedy and act out to explore. While a man is confident in his world and has no reason to even look at another girl.

A boy gets his feelings hurt because he can't handle the truth. While a man looks at his woman and says "that's why I love you".

A boy will be satisfied with kids and a baby mama. While a man takes pride in his life and makes you his wife.

A boy will post his wild escapades for social media likes. While a man doesn't kiss and tell for what lies behind his bedroom doors is between him and his wife.

In a boy's world he will always have drama because he deals with little girls. While in a man's world he is at peace because his priorities are in order and he knows what he needs.

You see the difference between a boy and a man. A boy has to grow up to be a man. While a man has already conquered the title of being "the man".

The man that has dreams and goals

and doesn't mind sacrificing to
conquer things.

The man that reaches for your hand
and ask you to be the other half
that he lacks. Ladies be sure to
know the difference between the
two...don't get upset if you choose
to be confused.

A boy is merely a child not yet
molded into the man he will
someday, hopefully be.

THE DIFFERENCE BETWEEN THE TWO: GIRLS VS WOMEN

A girl and a woman are nowhere near the same. Although at times both women and men can become confused. At times both women and girls answer to the same name.

A girl is more focused on what outfit to wear to 1st Friday and what time to get to the club. While a woman is looking for a soulmate and rather not waste time being stalked upon like a piece of meat by fake ballers and wanna be thugs.

A girl will have extra money and blows it all on material things like Jordan's, Louie, and Versace belts. While a woman is smart and instead of blowing her money she'll invest it in stocks, IRAs, and 401ks.

A girl keeps up drama and mess with young females. While a woman is about her business and strays away from meaningless conversations with simple minded girls.

A girl will get angry when her man is working too much but will demand that he continues to pay for stuff. Always yelling what time are you getting off. A woman understands the pressures of her man and encourages and supports for someday she knows he will be his own boss.

A girl will always search for a guy to take care of her. While a woman works hard and prides herself on having things in her name.

A girl will be just fine being his baby mama or his old lady. But a woman will not settle for just being his lady or carrying his baby.

A girl will be fine with broken promises, teddy bears, necklaces, and things. While a woman will not settle without a ring.

Not just any ring…a ring that signifies a lifetime commitment between husband and wife.

You see a girl has dreams and talks about all the simple things she wants out of life. While a woman sets goals and timelines for she knows if she works hard her dreams will become reality.

Reality where she can live comfortably with an infinite salary.

"Some memories never fade"
-Unknown

DISTANT DAD

I walk around the house trying to figure somethings out. It's just me and my mom…something's not right.

I don't want to stir up anything so I won't ask mom, but I think I remember having a daddy.

Every Saturday mom leaves going to see someone…I ask mom can I go…she said "no son I don't want you to know about this road".

Sitting here thinking what road is she afraid, I'll go.
Being the bright young man that I am I ask do you know where my dad is?

Instantly, she began to cry. Now someone told me when a woman cries usually she's hurting deep inside and you should lie and say "everything will be fine".

I said "Mom why are you crying, I will stay here it's not a problem". She grabbed my hand and said "son let's go".

The road we traveled was a long journey, not one word was spoken only simple glances and light smirks.

Finally, we arrived…still confused. I see this building surrounded with wires and tall towers.

My mom leans over and kisses my face and says, "Son I only kept this from you because I love you. I didn't want you to see him this way. You know somethings are better left unsaid".

Before she could finish I interrupted and said "can I go in alone, I'm almost grown and I think it's time that my father and I have a conversation even if it's through a glass on a phone.

She smiles and gives the okay. "Good afternoon sir, I need you to empty out your pockets and walk this way".

"Whew, this is really a cage, mama don't ever have to worry about me coming to this place".

Sitting in this chair not knowing what to expect this guy walks in from the other side and immediately begins to smile as if he were expecting me.

"Hey son, how have you been, you've grown up so much looking just like ya old man…hey when I get out of here things are going to be fine…we're going to go here and we're going to do this".

I interrupted "hi, I'm lost for words, but I need to say somethings before the guard comes back and tells me it's time to leave" , "I heard you don't get out for another four or five so you've honestly missed most of my life.

I'm 16 now and I just don't understand: the definition of a dad is just a man with a little more responsibilities, you're a poor excuse of a man if you can't handle that".
"Son when I get out I'm going to make up for all the years I missed".

"Man you can't you weren't there on my first day of school, you never told me that a woman is a jewel, never had anyone teach me how to stick up for myself, that's crazy but I'm not done yet".

"Mama did the best she could teaching me how to be a man, but from a woman's point of view so I explored on my own...since I didn't have you".

No one there to teach me how to treat a lady.
So I went by what I saw. You see I lost my virginity at a young age...that's how we get down nowadays.

But if a man had been in my life I would've known to wait until I made her my wife. But you couldn't cause you've been chilling in here.

So I continued being the stereotypical man "laying up" and "putting it down" all around town until I slipped up and now I have a

baby...don't get me wrong my son is a beautiful thing, but I would have never been in this predicament at this age if my father had taught me how to treat a lady.

I'm not going to sit here and talk about the why's, what ifs, or even cry about how you suck at this [fatherhood] 'ish, but I will say this I thank you for setting the perfect example on how I shouldn't be.

Poppa you taught me one thing. "What's that son"? "That a man and a father can be two separate beings, but until they are intertwined there will always be a thin line".

IF I COULD I WOULD

*If I could I would stop time today
just for a moment to rectify change.
If I could pause time just for a
second; I would rewrite our legal
and school system to help our
people from getting lost in
transition.*

*If I could I would rewind
time…flashback when unity was the
trend sticking together for mankind
because we all had liked minds.*

*If I could I would fast forward
through the hate, pain, and
trending topics of hashtags for
names.*

*If I could I would stop world
hunger…all the money we spend on
Jordan's and politicians. There is
no way this should still be existing
in our system.*

*If I could I would help all race
understand we all have one
life…what sense does it make to
fight.*

*Wishful thinking…who am I
kidding. If I could I would stop
Time today just for a moment to
incite some change.*

RACE

*When you look inside my hand
…what color do you see?
We were all created one in the
same.*

*The only difference is the melanin
of my skin.
I remember what Dr. King use to
say, "one day".*

*Yes, one day a black boy and white
girl can hold hands and play*

*But no one mention that one day
the inside of the black man's
Hands would be almost irrelevant.*

*Only the flip side that show the true
color of his skin would serve his
relevance.*

*I wish we could also say I pledge
allegiance to the Nation where we
are all created equal*

*Yes black, blue, white, yellow or
purple we were all created to exist
in this circle of life.*

BACK IN THE DAY

Thinking back in the days when we were young some days I sit and wish we were kids again because those were the times.

I remember those days the six of us ran this so called game…mess with one get ready to run 'cause we would all be there. We are our sisters' keeper and that isn't just some cliché quote.

Inside jokes that no one else could understand, laughing in public had people watching and wondering.

People always asked how are you girls so close…don't you guys get on each other's nerves.

When no one understood why one of our attitudes changed…just know the sisters always had a plan of action to make sure things were okay.

Though we've grown we will never depart…bloodline through thick and thin.

Back in the day when we were young I remember how we loved each other so much we would sacrifice our life…well almost we would simply sacrifice our backside.

When one got in trouble we all shared the pain.

Sometimes I sit and wish we were young again so we could just sit, talk, and laugh all day.

IT WILL BE OKAY

Sorrow, hurt, and pain is sure to come, but don't worry the battle has already been won.

Don't worry about him; he has graduated to a better place. A place where no harm or sickness can be in his way.

It's all right to cry because someone has to hurt sometime. But remember troubles don't last always.

So you must do what you have to do to continue living your Godly ways.

He is smiling down on you saying "Son wipe your face I am blessed being in such a place, kiss your mother and tell her I

Love her. "Be sure to always do what's right and never let God out of your sight".

Dedicated to Pastor Ellison for Papa Ellison

SUNRISE TO SUNSET

Sunrise to sunset, God only guarantees the last breathe. Please don't weep for my time has come.

The Lord got tired of watching me run. To you my son, I am still near.

Just sit back and listen to my voice in your ear. To my daughter, daddy is okay.
Always remember God will make a way. So I say to you, begin to pray. Please don't sit and grieve over my body. As for my soul…God already got it.
It's okay to cry, the heart needs that sometimes. Look up to the sky you will then see me upon cloud nine.
Lift your head up and tell the Lord thank you. For allowing me to become one of his angels.

Everything will be okay, because troubles don't last always.
From sunrise to sunset, until we meet my soul shall rest!

Dedicated to Terry and Kim for Uncle John

USE TO BE

I use to stay on your case always
Pushing you away.

But no matter what you always seem
To keep me in a safe place.

Oh how I use to be, but now
All of that has changed.

I have graduated and I am now
In a different range.

How I use to be is now no more
That old me is rotten to the core.

For I am soaring toward a higher
Limit. This is the new me

Can't you see!

NOBODY TO SOMEBODY

Everyone keeps telling me I'm something.
Is that statement really true?
If it is how can people be so cruel?

Many people say I'm something while others say
I'm nothing how could that be?
I know back then blacks were nothing, but the
Whites were always something.

I thought now we were equal, but no this is just the
Sequel, the sequels of back then coming back now.

I am something no matter what everybody says.
I will amount to something one of these days.

I will no longer be in pain for those people who say I'm nobody truly wish they were somebody!

A FRIEND I CHERISH

You told me many times that you would be there for me through thick and thin.

That's a true definition of a down for life friend.

No one can compare to the chemistry we have I know when times get rough you will always have my back.

Little did you know that's something I use to lack...true friends.

I didn't have anyone to confide in. Even when I was in sin you never condemned.

I'm sitting here ready to cry because we've known each other most of our lives.

And it's almost time to say good-bye to the good ole times and start over brand new.

It's funny with all the females I claimed to be my friend you're the only one that continued with me to the end.

No matter how much we fight it's hard to stay mad at someone who was meant to be your sister, but God decided to make your best friend instead!

The prayer I use to pray when I didn't have anyone I thought I could depend on was, "Lord, if you send me just one true friend I will cherish our friendship until the end".

I can proudly say God heard my prayers because he sent you to be there to listen when I go through.

Yes, I know I may make you mad at times, but it's never intentionally trust me.

It's like you're the better half that I lack...if we were one person we'd be perfect.

You have so much potential and I truly look up to you, because you're not only true to your friends but you're true to yourself and that's something I wish I had.

IT'S OKAY...IT WAS TIME

August 24th I will always remember this day. I came up the elevator and my heart drop with pain.

Everyone kept asking me are you okay? This is crazy because I prayed the other day.

I asked the Lord to take the pain and have His way. You see on this day I came

Up to the 4th floor like I always do, to come see you. But this time when the doors opened my parents were waiting on me. It
Was like I felt a breath of wind come over
My body.

I felt you say "Brit my soul God already got it", but I was suddenly at peace because your pain was immediately ceased...you see I had this dream.

It seemed so real you told me you were tired and ready to go home but I didn't know what home. It was hard for me
To understand where you were going with the conversation and then that song began to play, "Let Go and Let God" like some revelation.

I guess that was your way of letting me know that today was
The day.

The Lord said He will never put more on one than they can bear. Everyone respected you because You based your life on being fair. You inspired so many while you were here and never showed a sense of fear.

The devil thought he won, but he needs to know God just Gained another one! I remember what you told me to tell the family...so here we go.

She wants you all to know don't stop keep on the go. You know what you have to do. Help each other out but please Don't cry over my body because God already got it.

I'm sitting here watching you all making sure you stay On task.

To you my son I know you won't let me down keep your family together no matter what may be going on.

Remember that song, "Keep on holding on". Make me proud my son.

To you my daughter my very first born. There's so much to say. You have made me so proud. I have set the foundation so now you need to build on it.

32

*Remember everyone has to hurt
and cry the soul needs that
sometimes. But you can't go
through life with watery eyes.*

*You're a strong successful woman
and it's time for you to recognize.
You have a daughter of your own.*

*Bring her up the way you were
raised in my home. I love you both
dearly keep mama strong this is the
time when she needs both of you in
her life.*

*To the rest of my family I am finally
at rest
God has said I've past my previous
test. You may be wondering why He
waited until now to take me.*

*I prayed a long time ago and I
said, "Lord don't take me
Until my family is whole". These
past few weeks I've never seen all
you come together as one. That
meant so much to me.*

*Even though I couldn't speak it was
a sight to see.
One last thing I want you all to
know
Keep me going on.*

*If you see someone in need think of
me, things not going right just
continue to fight, and whatever you
do keep God in sight!*

Dedicated to Johnnie Mae Sellers

I'M NOT WORRIED

Two, four, six, eight, I thank God for you each day. Before I close my eyes I pray to God to keep you alive.

No matter how much you have hurt me and caused me shame. I would never wish upon you pain.

I got mines so you will get yours in time. This is my life and I'm trying to make things all right.

So I refuse to be down and out. So I go about my day praying and thanking my God for making a way.

*"You were given this life because you're strong
enough to live it"*
-Unknown

WHEN I THINK

Every time I think of life all I want to do is cry. I'm tired of going through so much pain and I'm sick of dealing with

Constant shame. I'm ready to be through with life. I know life isn't fair, but I didn't sign up to be a part of this world.

I need someone to help me out. I cry and shout...what is it all about?

It feels as if someone has killed...as if I'm in a war. I'm just ready to close the door.

I struggle hard to do my best, but yet I fail and in one ear I hear the yells while in the other eye I see the cells.

Jail cells.

Praying to myself don't do anything stupid. I go on but not for long.

I cry and cry then lie and lie and all I hear is why? Why cry then lie...why not lie then cry?

You need a reason to lie and a reason to cry. So you answer that unanswered question.

Let this be a lesson. You can live a little, give a little, and die little or you can live big, give a lot, and die with happy

Thoughts!

LIFE

I came into this world as a small human being with big dreams, but at the same time I didn't know much about life at all.

As years began to past I found myself always being picked last even when I tried my best.

From that point it seemed like life was just a big test. I heard from others what life could be.

They stated that life can be full of misery and strife, but with the Lord in sight your future can be bright.

As I grew older I figured out the pattern and secrets to life. You have to remember to do what's right and never give up because

You have to do what you have to do to survive in this life!

HOLD ON

What is there to hold on to in this life? I'm so tired of the criticism, lying, joking, and other cruelty.

"Do unto others as you would have them do unto you", doesn't mean much to the people here on Earth.

I just don't understand why can't I retaliate. Then I hear a voice telling me to hold on.

Sometimes I feel like some people just want to come and take my place because of all the hurt and pain they push toward

My way. Jealously and hate causes so much shame today. No matter what I can't give up because it will seem that I have

Given into my enemies. So I can hold on a little more and next time pain and anger comes knocking at my door I will simply

Walk away. Because with God I can hold on some more.

THE TIME OF MY LIFE

Tick tock goes the clock. The times of my life flash by. Let's see how I will choose to die.

I endure many struggles in my life and I'm simply too tired to fight.

I'm about to go to bed as I reach to turn off my light…I say to myself…two, four, six, eight…how many Tylenol will it take?

I know this is wrong…I'm sorry mom you're just too late. I'm about to cut myself a little deeper and deeper to see how

Much blood I can make. Dad you had no idea that's because you were always too busy.

You just missed it I drank this whole bottle now I feel a little dizzy.

Tick tock goes the clock. The times of my life flash by. I jump in the car and take my last ride.

An emotional wreck I cry out loud, "am I ready to die"? Without thinking I take that dive.

As I'm sinking my conscience decides to come alive and says, "It's okay to survive".

Quickly drifting away from the light. I hear people yelling, "Are you alright"?

I wish I could answer them but they're simply out of sight. The times of my life flash by.

Tick tock goes my clock. I hit rock bottom…so now my time STOPS!

The Real Deal: The Journey

Brittney J. McCurry

The Real Deal: The Journey

Edited By: Dr. Tammie McCurry

Copyright©2016 Brittney McCurry

ISBN-13: 978-1535483209 (CreateSpace-Assigned)
ISBN-10: 1535483202

Printed in the United States of America.

LAST RIDE

Friends don't let friend's drink and drive. Sit back and let me give you the reasons why.

Momma use to always ask me did I enjoy my life because if I did I should never drink and drive.

Being a teenager that was a hard line to abide by. One night some friends and I decided to go out and party.

Before I left my house I kissed my mom and dad…they said I love you and be safe tonight.

Ready to party I remembered what momma said, "Don't Ever Drink and Drive".

When we got to the party it was so live. I mean the music was right and everybody was hype.

Man, I love my life…I really had a good time tonight. My girls and I are now ready to proceed.

We get in our separate cars so we can leave. Heading to our designated homes this car decides to swerve in the "NO PASSING ZONE".

I'm now lying here all alone in the middle of the road. I'm on the

ground making a whimpering sound.

Lord please…I'm not ready to go now. The paramedics have now arrived.

I hear them talking as if I'm not alive saying, "We should call her parents now because she is going to die".

I'm fading in and out but before I go Mr. Paramedics could you let my folks know…

When my parents arrived they were a second too late. But wait the paramedics had something to say.

"Mom and Dad I know your sad, but don't be I'm on my way to heaven to be with our King. Of course mom I enjoyed my life…

That's why I didn't drink and drive. I'm sorry I couldn't stay to say good-bye but if I had one wish…

I wish someone had told those other kids drinking does end lives.

Well I'm glad I gave you guys that kiss, but mom and dad I must reminisce…because I wanted to stay alive so why did

I have to die? You see this is why
friends don't let friends drink and
drive because innocent people lose
their innocent
LIVES!

BECAUSE OF YOU

*You just don't know how much you
have impacted my life. Because of
you I learned that it's alright to
cry.*

*You taught me that I have no
reason to lie. I know now that I
don't have to beg for friends
because they won't be there in*

*The end. When I was ready to give
up you were there to stop me. When
I wanted to do something crazy you
were there to*

*Save me. I can truly say you have
my back through thick and thin.*

*Our friendship is deeper than our
skin. I know you always try to be
the bigger person.*

*Because when I do cry you try your
best to keep it bundled inside.*

*When I'm angry and don't show it
you make sure the world knows it.*

*Thanks for being who you are to
me.*

IF I ONLY HAD A CLUE

*I needed a few clues so I went to
someone I thought I knew.
I needed a hand and I couldn't ask
a man because I knew*

*He wouldn't understand so I tried
talking to this wo-man,
I thought maybe she would
understand.
We spent time together as if we
would be there for each other
Forever. I thought I knew what I
was getting into.
Maybe she wasn't the person I
thought I knew; if only I had a
Few more clues.
I thought I knew this person better
than that; so why would she
Go and hurt me so bad.
I guess that's what happens when
you try something new. What works
for others may not work for you.
If I only had a few more clues*

THE TEACHER

*I never knew you before this. But I
want you to know you're a gift.*

*I connected without thinking for a
second. It was like you were sent to
me from heaven.*

*You're always there for me
especially when I don't believe.
How could you be so sweet to a
person like me?*

*You're always happy, never
lacking, without acting you're
always real.*

*You came into my life right on time,
just to see if I was doing fine.*

*I know God knew what He was
doing when He introduced me to
you.*

*It's funny you, my teacher are
always there when I go through. I
know when I feel I may have no one
else.*

*I can always count on you. When I
don't know what to do I can always
talk to you.*

*Thanks for keeping me on that
straight and narrow path when I
thought I would collapse.*

*I know now that life isn't fair, but
God will never put more on one
person than they can bear.*

*I appreciate you being there,
thanks for letting me know you
truly care.*

*What can I say "Favor Isn't fair"!
God said He would help, so He sent
me someone like you.*

BREAKING NEWS

Its 10:00 time for the news. Everyone gathered in the room. BREAKING NEWS came across the screen.

Unfortunately, Jennifer Greene has not been seen. "If you know anything, please inform me", her father said.

Next the news reporter read, "Johnny Lang is dead, the gang master, who love red.

"What is this world coming to", someone said. Another child is raped...and dead.

"For heaven's sake", grandma sighed. The last news line was up next.

What else is left? Suddenly the news lady seemed very hesitant. "This just in", "God said He will forgive you for all your sins if

You just give in, turn your lives around". There was no sound in the room.

The reporter said, "He will be coming soon and the majority will

be doomed, don't wait get on your knees and pray".

Then the news reporters looked at each other and said…WE'RE GOING TO BREAK!

I WONDER

I wonder why so many people nowadays are more afraid to cry than die.

I wonder should we have a website called www.dontlie, I wonder will telling the truth soon be a game that we play when

We are going insane. I wonder why so many people are afraid of the feeling of love especially from above.

I wonder is this really how life is supposed to be. Aren't families supposed to stay together and live happily?

I wonder will children always have to deal with the feeling of hurt and shame. I wonder will we walk up to our preachers and ask "Pastor, do you know my name".

I wonder will pedophiles be the new trending thing that society accepts…stating it is okay for Mr. to lust over little Mandy and ask for sex.

I wonder will our degrees and schooling soon be irrelevant. Will people rather flip$500 to make a quick hustle?

I wonder will drugs and thugs take over our communities making our

children believe this is the American dream.

I wonder where this road will take us and how it will end.

I wonder!

DON'T BE FOOLED

*It's hard nowadays to speak exactly
what you have to say. Especially
when you continue to go through
constant*

*Turmoil and pain. Sometimes
situations make you feel insane and
have you thinking this stress is part
of the game.*

*Sometimes you can just get so
confused. You think you have won,
but don't worry God will show me
the sun.*

*When he does justice will be done.
How could you? Did you know I
looked up to you?*

*How could someone who is so
involved with the church turn
around and hurt me so much.*

*You don't understand how tough
this is. Every time I see your grin it
makes me sick because you think
you haven't committed*

*A sin. You men...well most of them
will never give up until you win.*

*Then when I speak my mind to you
all my hate spilling ---you give a*

*sick smile and say "it's not rape if
we pretend you were*

*Willing". What is there to do? I
can't believe this is true. Lord I
promise I have learned my lesson.*

*But I have a confession. Lord I'm
really beginning to drift away from
you.*

*I am so confused. I thought those in
the church were holy and true to
you.*

*Yet one of your servants has truly
hurt and threaten me. How could
this be? Please explain this to me!*

*I guess I was just too blind to see
everyone isn't who they claim to
be! Even with titles it doesn't wash
away the sin.*

THIS GIRL

Everybody thought her life was just right. She gave off the impression that she was just fine.

Little did they know she was falling apart inside. It began to get hard to hide the emotions being felt.

She just knew her problems would go away and things would get better someday.

So many ups and downs caused this young girl to walk around school with a frown.

Everyone would get on her, saying she is never happy. Little did they know that was something she was lacking.

The kids used to talk about her saying she just wants some attention but little did they know she wasn't looking for that

Kind of recognition. "Oh, you just want someone to feel sorry for you" is what people would say, but little did they know this

Girl was barely making it from day to day. You see she got tired of everybody talking about her life, always criticizing

That's not right. She had told a good friend of hers what was going on.

She told her she just felt like giving in. Even though it was a sin, the girl thought it over and over again.

See you never know what someone may be going through unless you take the time to ask.

You see this girl lived that "hard knocks life". Her mom was always strung out... trading tricks for dime bags.

Her dad well he was a sperm donor to be exact but that didn't prevent him from using his seed to meet his needs.

You see she had contracted HIV and had no one to turn to. Everyone just thought she was just some disturbed kid.

No one ever asked the simple thing are you alright? Her friend wasn't equipped to give her any advice.

Her good friend's voice was the last she heard because that day after school she took her life.

DECEPTION

*No matter how much you cry.
Those tears can't wash away the
stains from the inside.*

*People come and then they go. For
what, we may never know. It seems
like every time you try to do what's
right, you always*

*End up in the wrong someway. One
night this girl was laying in her
bed, just lying there playing the
thoughts in her head.*

*Suddenly, a friend of hers came
into the room. She ask the girl
could she come over to her house to
help her out.*

*Without thinking she agreed and
said no doubt. She got to the house
and something just didn't seem
right, but she shook it*

*Off and went on with the night.
Some guys came over unexpectedly.*

*The girl who she came over to help
had pre-planned this little set up.*

*Little did the girl know this was
only the beginning of one hostile
road.*

*The girl who only came over to
help… found herself in a situation
she could not get out of.*

*Trapped in a room with three guys
and her supposedly friend. They
took turns attacking her body. With
Aaliyah playing in the background
"Are you that somebody".*

*When everything was said and done
the guys had to make a run. The
girl's mother had then made it
home.*

*I told you this would be a long
road. They argued back in forth
about what had just occurred.*

*The other girl upset and hurt did
what she thought would work. She
lied to the girl's mother about the
incident and was able*

*To escape from the unstable
predicament. This girl learned a
valuable lesson; every time
someone needs your help…ask him
or her why can't they do it
themselves?*

*Everyone isn't your friend that
claim to be watch out for those
Lucifer's in disguise. They are
trained to deceive.*

SILENT CRIES: ELI

My name is Eli and I'm only two. I hear people around me saying I'm hyper active and I don't have a chance.

All mom's guy friends say mom should've given me away because she never wanted me anyway.

I can't talk that well...not yet; but I can point and yell. My mom has a new guy friend every week and none of them seem to like me. Week after week I have another bruised cheek.

This time momma got her a man that she seems to like he pays for everything and he even stays the night.

One night momma left me at home with her new man. I accidently spilled sticky stuff all over my hand. I went to tell Mr. and he pushed me into the fan.

I started crying because I hit my head. Then he yelled, "One more word and you are dead". I don't like it when people are mean so I began to scream.

My name is Eli and I was only two. I made my mom's boyfriend upset

so he threw me out the window of our apartment complex.

SILENT CRIES: JENNIFER

My name is Jennifer and I'm the big seven. I'm the only girl and I have two teenage brothers.

I usually play by myself because the boys hate that I'm a girl. I always ask can I play or can I go and all they give me are blank stares.

They say I'm spoiled because Me-Ma always gives me what I want. Oh yea, daddy and momma are no longer here they were in a bad accident and died last year.

Grandma hasn't been feeling well so she has been laying down to rest. My brothers were trying to sneak out but they knew I would tell.

We got to their friend's house and I knew I was too young to be there because there were no toys just older boys and lots of noise.

Sitting on the couch I saw my brothers give a man a big stack of cash…I laughed to myself I think they are probably buying me some more snacks.

The man came over and my brothers waved. The man said sweet girl what's your name.

My name is Jennifer and I was only the big seven when my brothers sold me into slavery.

No one will ever

find me because my pimp has redefined me.

<u>SILENT CRIES: BRIAN & BRIANNA</u>

I'm Brian and this is my twin sister Brianna and we're fifteen. We've been bounced around from various foster homes.

Our real mom is a prostitute and she belongs to the streets. She didn't really care about us only focused on her weed.

Well we ran away today our foster mom kept beating Bri and she would never feed me.

Out in these streets; me and my twin made the vow, "I take care of you and you take care of me".

One day a man drove by us on the corner; his name was Mr. Warner and he owned a troubled youth group home he said. He took us in and we smiled thinking our life was finally about to begin.

Well Mr. Warner ran an underground operation in his downstairs den.

My name is Brian and this is my twin Brianna and we're fifteen that day our names changed and our lives as our own was no more.

We are now here to serve you ma'am or sir and all your viewing needs. Betting all night if you want just tell us what you want to see.

Only fifteen and we were forced into a porn ring.

I'M SORRY

*Laying here with this empty feeling.
The people tell me I'm going
through a process it's called
healing.*

*The people around weren't willing
to give me...no...us a chance.*

*All they looked at were the
immediate facts. Yeah, it's sad how
the people close to you are glad
when something is taken away*

From you.

*I'm so mad...just so you know this
wasn't my choice. I had a little
voice on what your outcome could
be.*

*I can't help but cry because I
allowed the death of an innocent
life.*

*I'm thinking now even though I
know it's too late. What if I had put
up a bigger fight?*

*What if I ran away? Just maybe you
would still be a part of my life.*

*I know it's my fault and I truly
apologize, but I know that won't
bring you back into my life.*

*Just so you know it; if it were left
up to me you would still be
forming...yes inside of me.*

*I wanted you; I was ready to go
through whatever I had too.*

*Dear Lord, I didn't want this to
happen, but you are the captain so
I know you knew what you were
doing.*

*Do me a favor...take care of my
baby. Explain to him or her that
mommy didn't win...yes it was a sin
that will never happen again.*

*To you my child, I enjoyed your
presence for the little time we had.*

*Don't be sad you still have your
heavenly dad who will be there for
you no matter what.*

*Even though I was unable to bring
you into this world, mommy will
always love you my unborn boy or
girl.*

3:00 PM

You tell me you love me oh so much. I don't understand why you would allow me to go through so much stuff.

I'm sorry I just can't see it because when I pitched a fit you still made me go through with it.

I don't understand why you are so judgmental of me. Everyone makes mistakes because God made us that way.

The situation wasn't even my fault. Even though that's not what you thought.

Yes, I admit I lied to you to help someone else out. So now that gives you the right to force me to take an innocent life.

Do you see what you're doing to me? I cry now every time the clock strikes three.

You ask why three because that's the time I had to give up what was forming inside of me.

I have nothing more to say to you. My life changed greatly on that Saturday.

Yes, I have to say you got me acting this way. Not once did I hear "daughter are you okay"?

How about "I still love you". I couldn't get a word...nah you probably just stood and observed.

You see that hurts because I just sacrificed my baby's life to only get the silent treatment from you too.

This isn't right. You got me over here hating my life. I'm a seventeen year old girl who had to give up a life in order to

Save hers!

COACHES MVP

*You always told me to be careful.
And I would hear you to some
extent, but I was too hard-headed
to take the hint.*

*So I guess someone had to teach me
a lesson since I just didn't want to
listen.*

*I'm so sorry I didn't call on you I
was so afraid and confused on what
to do.*

*I was hurt and dumbfounded...by
myself...no one around.*

*I drove home in tears with a
tremendous amount of fear.*

*I wasn't sure if I should tell you or
a friend of the situation I was just
in.*

*I thought it was ironic that I got to
come and see you out of the blue
and you told me you loved me, then
this person ...*

*Coincidently, knew I was out and
wanted me to drop by his house.*

*Well, you know me...rarely think
twice before encountering this
thing called life.*

*I thought nothing of the phone call.
I went to see what it was he wanted
to see me for, I stepped in the house
and he closed the door.*

*I asked where everyone else was
since the house was completely
empty.*

*He told me ...then he told me to
come up stairs so he could show
me.*

*Still being me, I'm thinking I will
sit in this chair and eat my ice
cream then when I finish I can
leave.*

*Yeah right...funny...jokes on me.
Sitting there chilling watching the
game.*

*I noticed at the corner of my eye
this... this guy, meeting my eyes.*

*So what's up, we started talking
about the reasons for me coming
over..."Okay cool".*

*"I've missed you". As I looked up
at him this was not a normal
statement being made since he was
my coach and sees me every day.*

*I laughed then turned back to the
TV. Then he said, "It's like that
now"?*

*I didn't know what he was referring
to then he told me to come sit on
the bed so I could help him pick out
somethings.*

*There again me being me I moved
from the chair.*

*Then another random statement
was made. "You're the only girl
other than my main girl I've had in
my room… in my bed…that's good
isn't it"?*

*I looked and said yea but anyways,
I'm about to go.*

*So he reached his hand out in a
position of a handshake…so I
reached for the handshake but then
it was too late.*

*I ended up on my back in the bed
with him rubbing his hands on my
head.*

*"What's wrong with you, get off of
me", I said.*

*He looked me up and down and
said your body is so small but I
know you're not a virgin at all.*

*I told you I missed you and I was
serious.*

*"Please don't do this, let me go".
"No, you're here and I'm
ready…I'll go slow".*

*I could not move. I had no choice
but to lose.*

*It was like a game of spades he was
determine to get laid.*

*He had the ace of spades while I
only had the queen of hearts it was
too late.*

*Not again I cannot win. Even when
I stay in the right something always
seems to come and ruin my life.
After everything happened I slowly
got in my car. My inner thighs were
hurting and my eyes were burning.*

*With tears flowing down my face I
started on my way back to my
place.*

*All the way home, my thoughts
were just blank. I glanced at the
time and it said it was 12:00
o'clock in the morning.*

*Frantically shaking I thought what
do I do…we have a game to today
and the person who scares me the
most will be coaching me today.*

BATTLING WITHIN

*I have an announcement and a
concern....so listen up and read
this definition so maybe you will
learn...*

*"A person who feels hatred for,
fosters harmful designs against, or
engages in antagonistic activities
against another; an adversary or
opponent", now tell me what that
means...*

*Sitting here thinking I know this
can't be right. Saying to myself I
know this wrong is certainly not
pleasing in God's sight.*

*Asking myself what am I doing?
Trying to figure out exactly what
I'm pursing. Let me ask you this did
you know enemies come and go...
even though you learn to live and
deal with them along the road.*

*Have you ever felt like who do you
call when you've given your all?
Most people would say they make
you stronger when they try to make
you fall.*

*But do you recall having the
"worst enemy" ...the one that
knows you ...flaws and all.
Continually, praying on your knees
saying "Lord rescue me"...but
your cry for help feels like a
dropped call.*

*They use what they know about you
as a weapon of their own...the*

*stare in their eyes seems so cold.
Making it seem like the devil has
your soul.
Do you know what it's like to be
alone...sometimes your enemy will
remind you and take control.
Making you believe you should take
the opposite road.*

*Have you ever had an enemy that
deceives you to do things you know
you shouldn't do. How do you deal
with a battle that seems
unbeatable?*

*It's kind of like AIDS ....incurable
or maybe like a disease that's just
untreatable.*

*You see sometimes you get tired of
fighting all the time. Sometimes you
feel like giving in is better than
being let down when you don't win.*

*Some may say walk away; others
may say confront them and go on
about your day.*

*Tell me what do you say when
you're in a battle with someone you
felt you knew...Tell me what do you
do when your worst enemy is you?*

A LESSON LEARNED

Once upon a time there was a young girl; confused and angry because she didn't sign-up to be a part of this world.

She wasn't your average eighteen year old. You see in her life she carried a heavy load.

A lot of people did not know the things she had to go through. People would see her and say you have it all together, but little did they know behind closed doors her life was filled with bad weather.

She tried to hide those not so good feelings telling herself things will get better. What lays behind a smile for her an expression that had been there a while.

You may be wondering what caused her to be so sad. She was alive that was a reason to be glad. Yes, that statement is true, but let me ask you a question what would you do if you were in her shoes?

Would you be able to look at yourself in the mirror and say "I love you"; after your innocence has been stolen away from you. From a man that tried to run game and the worst part you didn't even know his name.

Well could you look at your child with a smile remembering the awful way they were conceived. Can you believe this is happening to me she once said.

In fact what if some guy came along and said he loved you. What is there to do, but say "hey I love you too"? Then he turns around and hurts you.

You find yourself in a situation again saying to yourself no this is my child I will carry it until the end.

How do you deal with constant turmoil and shame? "Sometimes I wish I could die and come back with a different name".

YOU DESERVE TO KNOW

What have I done? You didn't deserve this. Your life was just fine that is until I intervened and took you on this "wild ride".

You just don't know how much you have impacted my life. Because of you I learned that it's okay to cry.

I must thank you because sometimes I don't know why I do the things I do. You see in my life I've had many people come and go. I've heard of seasonal beings, but I'm just waiting on that lifetime angel.

You see I never knew you before this, but I want you to know your gift. I connected without thinking for a second. It was like you were sent to me from heaven.

Without hesitating I told you my life. Without judging you told me everything will be alright.

You see I've been having a little trouble finding myself, but when I look into the mirror I see the reflection of someone I want to live up to be. I know no one is perfect, but I think God has molded you close to be.

I honestly can't believe God let me trust in someone I barely knew. I had no clue, but I'm so glad it was you.

Your smile and the look you have in your eyes gives me the drive not to hide. You see I've never felt this way so I think I should let you know.
Never have I felt someone cared so much for me. Everyone has always been concerned with what I do or what I've done but never taken the time to actually see what was wrong.

I'm sure God would be pleased and will grant you all your good deeds for putting up with me.

I prayed the other day and I said Lord on judgment day if you would allow it "let me wait" before I enter the gates...when he ask me why I said I want to enter the gates with the woman who saved my life.

That was a horrible night...I wanted to let go and simply give in. I felt I had no purpose and I was simply taking up space. Tears rolling from my face I looked in my phone and saw your name.

*The inner me saying give it one
more try and I continued to cry. I
texted you and told you I was
through not knowing you would not
rest until I made the right decision.*

*You help me understand that life is
so worth living, and by giving in I
was just allowing the devil to win.*

*I know I can be a bit much to put
up with but someone once told me
"your biggest challenge can be
your greatest Accomplishment".*

THE FINALE

*Have you ever told yourself you
wouldn't do something again...?*

*You told me you loved me and from
jump I felt it was true. What else
could I do but let my guard down
and open up to you.*

*I told you my other relationships
just didn't last and with a straight
face you said don't compare me to
your past.*

*From that point I felt comfortable
with you...I told myself he might be
the one I say "I do" to.*

*I remember the saying "some
things are too good to be true", but
I thought nah not you.*

*But here we go again ...I find out
that you have a child...wow...that's
wild...I mean what man denies his
seed.*

*But because I love you I stuck
around. You promised me again
there were no more loose
ends...being me I fell for it again.*

*You told me I was your world yes
me I was your only girl. Silly B*

*"tricks are for kids" and the joke
fell on me.*

*Can't you see I thought this was
built on trust...but it seems it was
all lust. Why did I sleep with you?
Now a part of me is lost within you.*

*Maybe this will work B don't give
up so easily I said. So things got
better but I spoke too soon. I forgot
to watch the news it said more bad
weather would be here soon.*

*Who are they? And how do they
know my name? I'm sorry but I am
grown I don't play childish games.*

*Why can't I just walk away? I mean
it would end all of this drama if I
just go my way. But being me I
decide to stay.*

*Okay seriously this is your last
chance. Because remember there is
no ring on my left finger.*

*Let me ask you this "self why are
you putting up with this"..."girl
don't you know there are more men
you just have to be careful what sea
you throw your rod in".*

Okay, why am I with you again...oh yes because in the beginning you stood out from the rest. Yes you were the one that approached me correct.

You made promises to me that were so simple to keep. You only had to be sure not to hurt me but you failed at that miserably.

Let me tell you something and I want you to listen well. I was foolish enough to let you mess up more than once and take me through hell.
But now I have to look out for the person who is most important ....me. I love you but I can't allow you to damage my heart anymore.

You see my heart works for me...it's the most important organ that lives in my body. It works hard to keep everything functioning inside of me.

So this is it...if you can't handle my heart with delicacy please let me be. I will respect you more as a man if you set me free.

I want this to work honestly I do...because I told you I love you

those words will forever be true. But like the song said "her name is me and I love her more than you will ever know"...so if you make me choose between the two...sorry baby but I don't choose you.

So now it's your turn to choose ....!

IT'S YOUR LIFE

*Never rush life whatever you want
will come in time. Don't get in a
hurry to grow up because that road
is rough.*

*Make sure you find the right one
not the one you think you love.
Always have respect for yourself
treat your body like the temple it is
and girls be careful who you let in.*

*Never surrender in the fight until
the end and you will win. I say
again choose your friends the ones
who will stick with you*

*Until the end. No matter what they
will never turn on you always being
there when you're going through.*

*Never be afraid to let go and when
something isn't going right simply
say no.*
*Don't let people influence you to do
things that you know aren't right
because remember it's your life.
SO LIVE IT!*

HOW COME?

*I just don't understand what I could
have done that was so bad. That
would make you so mad.*

*I just don't understand why not just
take something from me like
something I don't really need.*

*Yet you turn around and take my
friends and family. What are you
saying?*

*They don't deserve me? This is
crazy I really need someone to save
me and take me out of this horrible
fairy tale.*

*This can't be sensible to go through
this much hell. If that wasn't
enough you made my road
extremely rough.*

*I experienced things that I thought I
would never go through. But you
proved me wrong so I sit and cry
my little song.*

*"Where did I go wrong"? "Why
did I have to be the chosen one"?*

*I just don't understand why me, I
thought you truly loved me!*

<u>HELP ME UNDERSTAND</u>

"Why" are you leaving me? "Why" are you leaving me over this man? I just don't understand "why" over this man.

I miss you already are you sure you're ready. This is like a new beginning of life. A puddle of tears I fear because you won't

Be near. You're still a call away but it will never be the same. You fuss and fight ask yourself is this what you want in life.

Life does not have to be like a knife and hurt so badly. It's your life and you can choose the path of heartache.

If that's the route you want to take. I will always love you and that will never change, but the picture still remains the same.

No matter how far away you may be. I still don't understand "why" you left me over this man!

"Faith is like Wi-fi it's invisible but it has the power
to connect you to what you need"
-Unknown

FINDING MYSELF THROUGH YOU

*Words cannot express what needs
to be said. Me telling you thank you
will never be enough for things you
did.*

*I remember asking the Lord to have
mercy on me and
To send me someone who
understands me...like a human
being but really an angel designed
just for me.*

*Then you came into my life right on
time. Never would
I have thought I would open up to a
person like you. The Pastor's
Wife...always there when I seem to
be going through.*

*When I first began to talk to you the
spirit of hesitant
Suddenly went away. You started
speaking to my situation
Saying Lord make a way.*

*Without thinking twice I started to
share with you the things
That happened in my life and
without saying much you smiled
and said everything is going to be
alright.*

*You helped me realize that this too
shall pass and giving up
Would only satisfy the devil and
make him laugh.*

*I remember you saying this is a lot
to deal with as I looked in your*

*eyes I saw something inside. This is
how I knew you were sent to me.*

*When I needed love you were there
to give it. When I needed someone
to
Care you let me know you will
always be there. Must be true when
it says favor ain't fair.*

*Many people would have left me to
figure things out on my own, but
you stood right beside me making
sure I did not let go.*

*I remember many times that I
wanted to give up even when I knew
it was a sin but you wouldn't let
me...for you knew if I failed you
failed and you knew that wasn't the
Master's Plan.*

*How can I thank you enough for
lending me your help? I never felt
this way before; you helped me
open and close some doors.*

*With that said, I love you dearly
and that will never change just
As long as you stick with me. I
know God will continue to make a
way.*

DEAR LORD

Dear Lord I've been meaning to talk to you. Talk to you a little more than usual.

I don't want you to think I just come to you when I'm going through but I wholeheartedly would like to get to know you.

I want to know you like I know my friends. What makes you smile and what makes you cringe.

Sometimes I feel when I'm not living right that I dare not come to you.

But I would like to say I thank you Lord for who you are and what you are.

Though I may be distant I know without you there is no existence.

Thank you for not condemning me in spite of my flesh. Your mercy is amazing and I'd be crazy not to acknowledge you.

Teach me how to be a better me. Teach me to be the son or daughter you destined me to be.

I just want to make you proud so on that day you don't turn away.

Lord one day I hope to finally get to see your face at the pearly gate.

THANK YOU

Thanking you is our way of glorifying you. Your Revelations are crystal clear of what you want us

*To do. Your secret plan is not to intimidate man
But to see if we can live on this land.*

*Don't get it wrong my Lord is strong. We shouldn't
Be working on fighting and killing each other*

*But concentrating on how to love and teach one another.
Lord we thank you for having so much trust.*

We just want to say thank you and while we are here on Earth we will continue to praise you.

THE MORNING KEY

Morning is the key to open the
door. Behind the door
Is the morning joy and glory.

Don't lose your key because you
only get one and
It opens all the doors.

The key symbolizes
God and how you let Him in.
He provides us with the morning,
glory and joy.

You might have trouble with
The locks because sometimes the
Lord has to change

The locks. If you walk right and
stick with Him; He
Will always leave the door
unlocked!

IT WILL COME

Healing is what I need I hope that
is your specialty.
Take all the pain and hurt away, I
pray to you each and

Everyday. Take your time and I will
continue to wait. If
I wait I know you won't delay.

For my healing is on the way. Lord,
I thank you for everything
You do. You bless me in so many
ways even when you might

Not want to. I will try to live right
but I cannot do it alone. I need you
just like Daniel. At times my life
seems to trap me in a lion's den.

Lord please continue to make a
way like you did for Moses and
parted the red sea. Sometimes Lord
I just need a clear path for me to
see.

I know everything I need will come
to me just like you did for Joseph
and all his dreams.

Yes I do believe in all your
promises. I'm even willing to wait
as Abraham did for I know at the
end of the day when I pray and
speak into existence it will come!

THE TEST

*Paying attention in church,
studying my bible, and taking notes.*

*I wake up in the morning and I
pray and get ready for whatever
test I have to go through.*

*This day has been hectic maybe I
should have ask some more
questions before you asked if I was
ready.*

*Lord I did my best but I just can't
comprehend why I have so many
tests to take.*

*I guess it wasn't my best. God can
you hear me I'm afraid I won't
make it to the next level if I can't
conquer the test you throw my way.*

*God says, my child I hear you but
remember the teacher is always
silent during the exam. Don't worry
you will receive all your extra
credit because I heard every outcry
from you.*

*Don't forget it's not cheating
because I gave the answer key to
you. Read my word and live by my
rules.*

*When you see your transcript you
will be amazed at how well you did
in school.*

HEAVEN

*As I look up into the sky I can see
myself flying high. That will be the
day when master says, "go make
someone's day".*

*I promise I will be the best angel
there is to be. God I promise I
won't let you down just wait and
see.*

*Things happen for a reason and I
can truly say it was worth it. I got
to heaven and guess what I'm
daddy's favorite little girl*

*And I'm really sitting on top of the
world! I have no more sorrows and
no more pains.*

*I guess it's true you have to lose to
gain. You might not get yours when
you want it, but trust me you will
get it in time!*

CHURCH

*Hallelujah, Praise the Lord, Thank
you Jesus. You saints scream at the
top of your lungs, but he has yet to
preach or*

*Sing one word to a song. "Excuse
me sir, why are you running around
the church"?*

*All the pastor said was that he was
able to buy himself a couple of
shirts.*

*Please ma'am tell me how this
works? Can the shepherd of the
flock just do what he wants?*

*How about this…Yes you Ms.
Secretary, is it okay to follow a
man who has destroyed his family?*

*It's okay you don't have to answer
my questions, but hey Mother;
living like this; will you go to
heaven?*

*You see church is supposed to be a
place where you go to make the
demons leave; yes a place where
your soul can be set free.*

*But can you believe it has turned
into a show. Somewhere everyone
wants to go to simply see how
exciting the people*

*Can be. Sitting there shouting and
falling out for a "MAN", who isn't
living what he is talking about.*

*Please don't get mad, I'm only
going by what I see. That's why I
get on my knees and ask the Lord to
help me.*

*When it's all said and over with on
judgment day ask yourself will the
Lord say, "Well done my good and
faithful servant"*

*Or will He look at you and simply
turn away!*

<u>ARE YOU A CHRISTIAN?</u>

Are you Christian? What do you mean don't you see me when I sing.

Do you not notice every Sunday I scream and shout...I may even fall out!

Am I a Christian...what kind of question is that? Do you not recognize how hard I clap at every word spoken?

You can't help but notice me I leave my seat continuously just because I'm me.

Come on am I Christian did you not see me lay hands on that lady...she passed right out...cause I'm a Christian I always know what I'm talking about.

How could you insult a person such as me I drive my nice car and wear my nice clothes and shout on cue how could I not be a Christian to you?

I mean didn't you hear me say "God bless you" to that woman over there even though all she deserves is my blank stares she has some nerve coming in here dressed like that.

You remember when you walked passed me I told that man "don't worry God will make a way" even though I was thinking this man can't be saved.

Ha am I a Christian ...well I think so!

P.U.S.H

Wondering where did I go wrong.
Asking myself why does my life
have to be such a sad song.

Just thinking when will happiness
come along. I've made many
mistakes in my life, but yet I
manage to fight.

I endured many struggles, but not
once did I close my eyes and die.

Now, I'm wondering why? Why did
I hold on for so long?
To end up right back in the devils
arms.

I don't mean to complain but I
don't know what to do.
I got on my knees and prayed to
you.

Lord please help me understand
what is the purpose of going
through?

I feel my faith has ran out and this
is my last chance so please hear me
out.

I've search for the answers, but
now I know I cannot do this alone.

With that said Lord I'm down on
bended knee...please Father rescue
me.

~Pray.Until.Something.Happens~

A TURN AROUND...TO TURN AWAY

I'm Sabrina and this is my story.
Don't worry all is well even though
I'm heading to hell.

You see I kind of live that not so
good life. I was the female...the
female from the streets.

I slept around searching for
something deep to define me.
I was the one on the corner that
you drove pass everyday with such
a disturbing look on your face.

Yes that was me strung out that
night in the streets.
I was yearning for something so I
figured I would get high, maybe I
would find some peace.

I've done all the dirt that I could
do, but in essence I'm calling out
for help from you.

I saw a tag on your car one day it
said "there's no limit in God" then
your church's name.

That Sunday I pressed my
way...even though I knew I would
be so out of place. I came anyway.

I get to the door ready to turn away
and immediately these ladies
greeted me and ask "how are you
today"? I thought maybe this will
be okay.
I entered the church and found a
seat comfortable enough for me.

A lot of people wouldn't know but I
love to sing so I was excited to see
a praise team.

I will never forget the song "God's
Able" I think the verse said "don't
give up on God cause he won't give
up on you...HE'S ABLE".

Whew, I started to tear up and I got
all emotional inside.
Next thing I noticed the little usher
ask me was I alright...she passed
me a Kleenex and said "Sweetie
God has you in sight."

Service continued on I kind of felt
all eyes were on me since I was
wearing some tore up jeans and my
hair was streaked with green.

But I remember what grandma use
to say... "Come as you are baby
God does not discriminate".

Next up the people conducting the
pulpit had everyone going it was
pretty funny to me.

People were running and falling
out I was so confused about what
that was all about.

Time for more singing the choir got
up. I said to myself I think that's
something I want to do.

I said maybe "God maybe singing
in the choir will help me get closer
to you."

Now it's time for the best part of the service the preacher lady said

.

Now being me by this time I was ready to leave and head back to the streets…but I decided to stay and give preacher man a chance.

With lifted hands he prayed and gave thanks. Then ironically he said now turn to your neighbor.

Repeat after me "there's no limit in God". From that point I knew it was meant for me to stay.

The message for the day…you must get saved in order to feel safe.

No matter what you look like or where you're from, God said its time to come home my prodigal son.

The pastor then open up the altar for people to come. First a woman and man got up I assumed they had marital problems and they needed to be prayed through.

Then I saw some guys who came from the back they reminded me of some men who use to take "care" of me.

The whole time I'm thinking I can't do that. I have money to make so I'll be back on the street that would be wrong of me to go up there to be set free.

Then he said "faith without works is dead". There is one more I will wait because today is your day.

Next thing I knew I was standing in front of this man he grabbed my hand and said "you're in the right place at the right time…don't focus on leaving here trying to make another dime".

I smiled and cried all at once and he began to pray. I felt better people gave me hugs and told me they were glad I came.

Then this lady came my way and said you have to change your ways.

Being me I'm thinking "yes I look like I'm from the streets" but ma'am I just got set free.

I told her ma'am… I am… but could you tell me how I could be a part of the singing ministry.

I feel that it will help me in this journey. She quickly said "Well baby first I must pray for your soul".

She placed her hand on my stomach and I told her to let go. You see in the streets when people put their hands on you that means they want control.
No disrespect ma'am but I thought the pastor just prayed for my soul.

"Yes, yes I know...but I've been where you were before so I know what demons you have behind closed doors."

Excuse me what did you say...just forget I ask I won't be coming back anyway.

My face fuming with anger and pain, I turned around and told her thank you for turning me away.

I started back to my corner where I felt comfortable enough to just be me...no one around to judge cause everyone around looked just like me.

I stood there and thought man and I almost gave this up.

Now the moral to this tale is simple be careful how you approach the mortal soul...because the words you speak can damn a sinner's soul.

This book involved various subjects that should not be taken lightly. Often tin
we want help but are afraid to take the first step.

If you are in need of help the following resources will help you greatly whe
you find yourself in a predicament and you need to find a way out. Please don't be
afraid to use them.

*Also check your local listing for support groups, counselors, mentors, etc. We exis
together to assist each other. Don't be afraid to seek help*

National Suicide Prevention Lifeline:
1-800-273-8255

American Pregnancy Hotline:
1-866-942-6466

National Adoption Hotline:
1-800-923-6602

Rape & Incest Nat'l Network (RAINN)
1-800-656-4673

National STD Hotline
1-800-227-8922
National Domestic Violence Hotline:
1-800-799-7233

National Sexual Assault Hotline:
1-800-656-4673

SAMHSA's National Helpline:
1-800-662-HELP

AAAAA Recovery First
1-800-734-5192
www.recoveryfirst.org

Made in the USA
Charleston, SC
22 August 2016